Alexander

THE ISLAND BLACKHOUSE

and a guide to 'The Blackhouse'
No. 42, Arnol

Edinburgh
Her Majesty's Stationery Office

© *Crown Copyright* 1978
First Published 1978

No. 42 Arnol is held in trust for the nation by the Secretary of State for Scotland and cared for on his behalf by the Department of the Environment.

'The Blackhouse', No. 42 Arnol, is situated in the township of Arnol off the A858 road on the west side of the Isle of Lewis [map reference NB 311 493]. Access is by metalled roads through and to the north of the township.

Hours of Opening

April to September 9.30 a.m.–7 p.m.
October to March 9.30 a.m.–4 p.m.
The monument is closed on Sundays

Front cover: The peat fire, No. 42 Arnol.

Inside cover: A family at Balallan, Lewis [1934]. S. T. Kjellberg, by permission of the Göteborg's Historiska Museum.

ISBN 0 11 491372 2

CONTENTS

5 Preface: A Personal Impression

9 The Blackhouse at 42 Arnol
10 *the roof*
15 *walls, floors and hearth*
18 *layout and fixed features*
24 *drains*
24 *furnishings*

31 Blackhouses on the West Side of Lewis

35 Change and Conservatism

39 The Village of Arnol

43 The Economic Pattern

52 Crofting Tenure

55 Sources

1966 photographs show the croft at 42 Arnol shortly after acquisition; the 1968 and 1973 photographs show the subsequent renovations.

PREFACE: A PERSONAL IMPRESSION

In Arnol the modern stone and lime or concrete-block dwelling houses roofed with slate, corrugated iron or tarred felt lie alongside older straw thatched blackhouses. In such a township, a strong impression is given of looking two ways in time. On the one hand, there is the present that has not yet shaken down properly. On the other, there is the past, whose traces are still clear enough to suggest a much more functionally integrated system of communal co-existence. Yet this past too is very recent, for the linear arrangement of blackhouses and later houses along the roads in these crofting townships is little more than a century old. The previous settlement was much nearer to Loch Arnol and the sea.

Blackhouses seem more archaic than they really are. Their architecture and layout carry on traditions of a form of living and working that is infinitely older. This was what impressed itself most strongly during my first visit to 42 Arnol in May 1964, when the house was still occupied.

The single door in the long front wall led into an area where some brown hens were kept. Immediately opposite, a second door opened into the barn. On the right there was a door through to the byre, where a young beast lay in a stall, bedded on straw. To the left, the door opening to the living room was partly covered by a netting-wire frame to keep out the hens.

In the centre of the stone and clay floor, a fire of peat smouldered with a steady, red glow from which rose, not so much smoke, as a smoky shimmer of heat, with no chimney to draw it out. The flavour of burning peat filled the air with warmth, adding an evocative dimension to the atmosphere.

Here three generations lived together, all entirely Gaelic speaking when on their own, in the context of a blackhouse that provided ample warmth and

The old blackhouses, mostly roofless, lie parallel to the modern buildings by the roadside. The grain and hay are in the corn yards, the potatoes have been gathered, and the peat stacks have been built. *J. Dewar Studios.*

View of the croft from the back, prior to restoration [1966].

shelter. By day the kitchen was the centre for the everyday domestic jobs of the women—mending clothes, preparing food for themselves, the hens and the calves, washing dishes. But the evening was the great time, when the whole family re-assembled, and people dropped in, to sit in social relaxation round the fire, the focal point of the whole house. Relaxed, but not necessarily idle, for spinning, wool-winding and knitting kept the women busy and the men might wind ropes out of freshly pulled heather fronds, or mend a broken creel.

One of the family has described her house in a school essay, in a way that tells much of a young Lewis girl's attitude to her milieu:

'During winter, many neighbours come in each night. We form a circle round the fire and discuss many subjects. The fire can be built as high as you like because there is no risk of a chimney catching fire.

'Very often, after tea a cailleach [old woman] comes in for a ceilidh. You know just to gossip. I remember a few years ago, when my uncle was at home from Canada, people used to come every night. What times we had, singing . . . and many other sources of entertainment!

'During the summer many tourists come to see the house. They ask to see the three legged pot hanging over the fire.

'The blackhouse is definitely the cosiest you can find.' [*West Side Story*, 1964, p. 22].

There is here a sense of pleasure in social communion, a sense that came through clearly also on my day-time visit. Mingling with this, on my first sight of the blackhouse kitchen, was an awareness that this was a glimpse of a culture nearing its end, becoming part of the country's historical past.

Change is an inevitable part of life, to be accepted, not deplored, but it is important to understand and appreciate the main stages of cultural development. The kind of culture represented by the blackhouse was a very long and basic stage in the history of Highland and Island Scotland, and 42 Arnol will now remain [as a guardianship monument cared for by the Department of the Environment] an enduring symbol and reflection of a form of community organisation that in another generation or so will lie quite outside the memory of individuals.

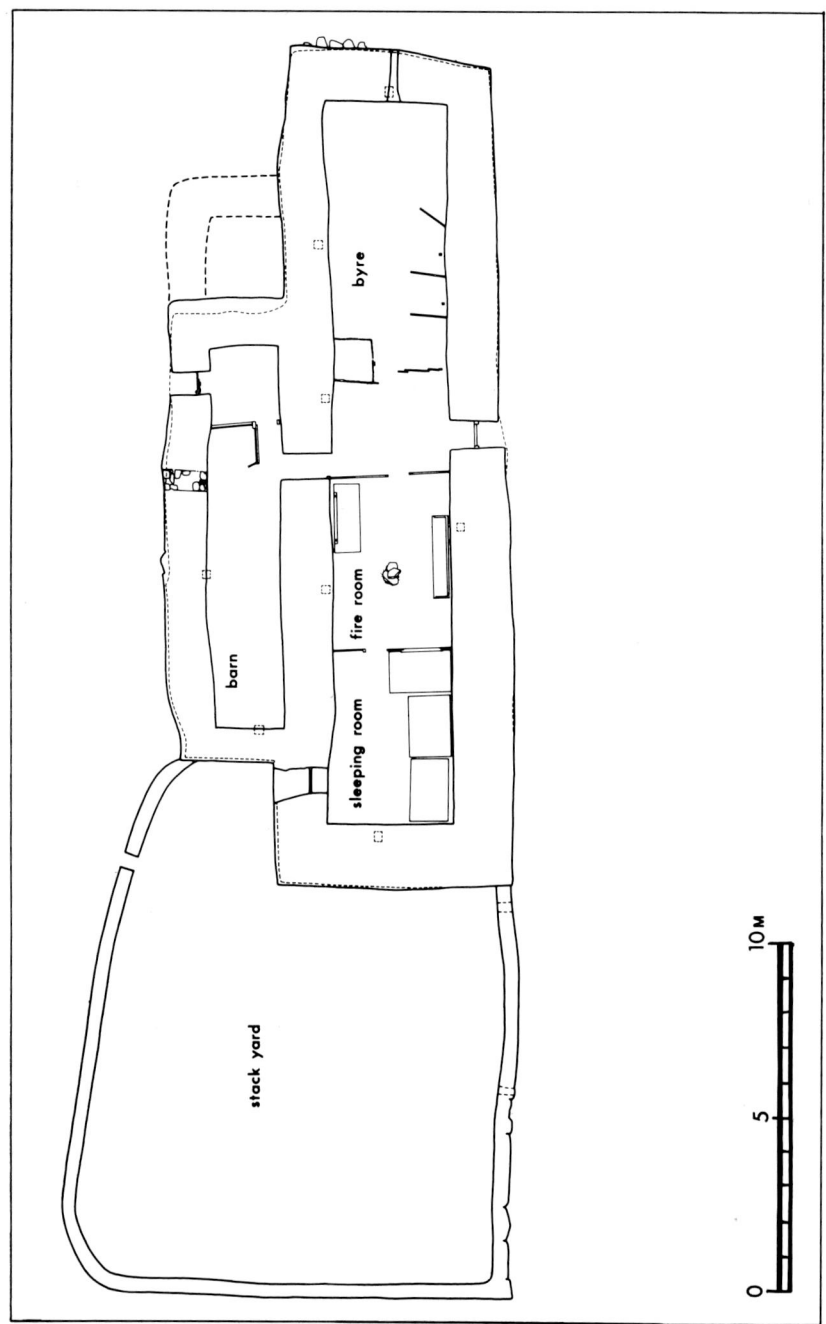

Fig. 1. Plan of croft and stackyard. The dotted outline gives the original extent of the barn. The dotted squares mark the rooflights.

THE BLACKHOUSE AT 42 ARNOL

Because of the transitional nature of the blackhouse at 42 Arnol, a study of its structural features throws a good deal of light on the history and social background of blackhouses in general on the West side of Lewis. As it stands, however, No. 42 is not exactly in its original form, since the barn has been shortened. The explosion of a land-mine *c.* 1940 loosened the wall at the south end of the barn, and a length of 3·7 m was dismantled. The present south gable is relatively recent and it is a comment on the nature of the building stone that no appreciable difference can be seen between this and the older walling. The outline of the original wall can still be observed opposite the peat-stack, and the part of the present house wall that was formerly the inner wall of the barn is built of rather smaller stones than the originally exposed surface beyond it at the south end.

The rear of the croft, showing the outline of the original wall of the barn [1973].

❧ THE ROOF

The present roof has been restored by the Department of the Environment. The rafters [Fig. 4], linked by single tie-beams, cross at the apex to make a cradle for the roof-ridge. The tie-beams are fixed by wooden pins to the rafters. The horizontal purlins are of separate lengths of wood lashed together, including a large oar or sweep in the rafters over the front door. In both house and byre there are upper and lower purlins, and base purlins low down near the wall-head [Fig. 5]. The barn, of which the roof is lower and narrower, has only upper and base purlins.

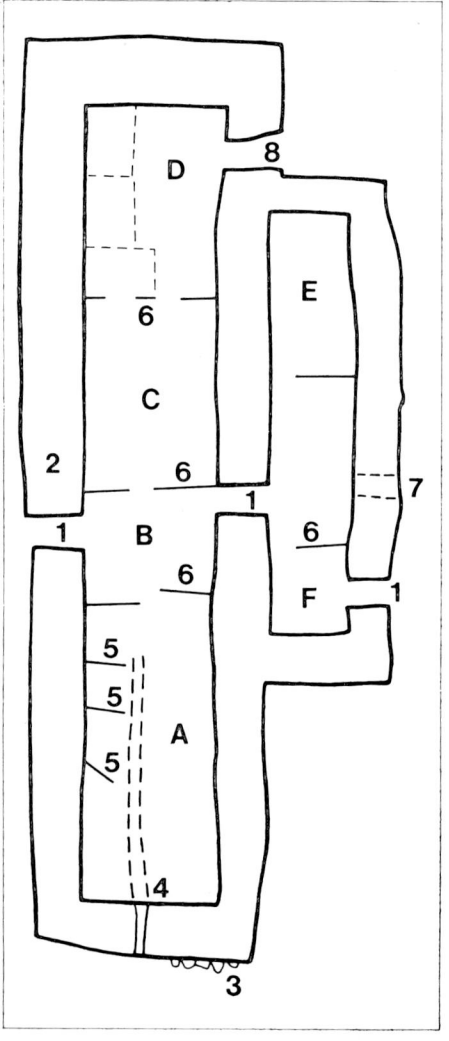

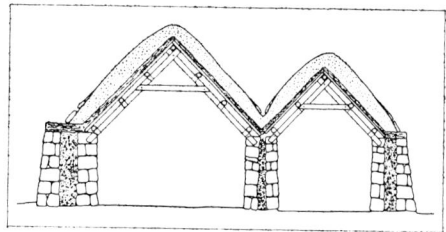

Fig. 2. Section through house and barn.

Fig. 3. Plan and fixed features: [A] *bàthaich*, byre; [B] *stairseach*, entrance area; [C] *aig an teine*, the living area; [D] *uachdar an tighe*, bedroom; [E] *sabhal*, barn; [F] *cùil-nan-othaisgean*, end of the barn (used as a shelter for lambing ewes etc.); [1] *dorus*, door; [2] *balla*, wall; [3] *staireachan*, stone steps leading to the roof-ridge; [4] *toll lodain*, wall opening for byre drain; [5] *buabhall-na-bà*, stall partition; [6] *tallan fiodha*, wooden partition; [7] *toll fhasgnaidh*, winnowing hole; [8] *uinneag*, window.

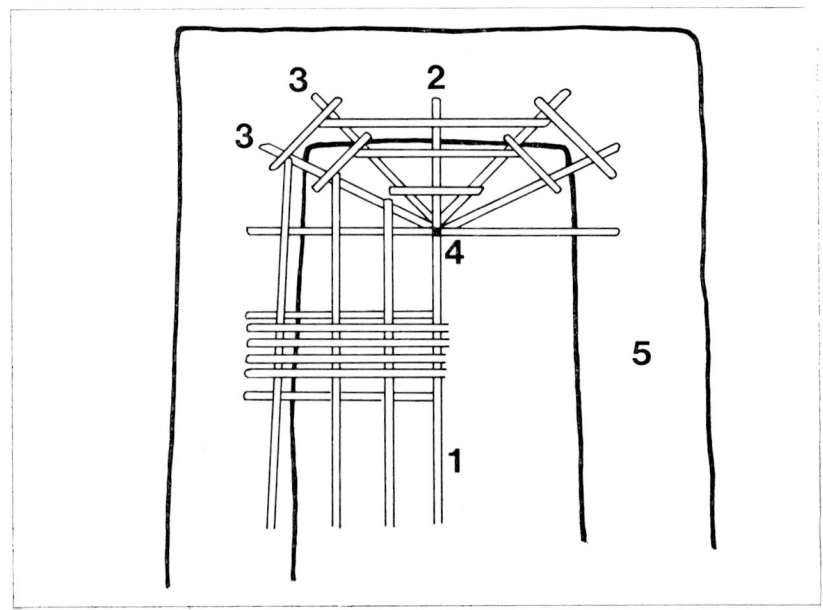

Fig. 4. The roofing timbers: [1] *gath droma*, roof ridge; [2] *a' chorr* or *corra-thulchainn*, central rafter or hip; [3] *roinn-oisinn*, corner rafters; [4] *maide fithich* or *corra-thulchainn*, protruding stick for ropes; [5] *balla*, wall.

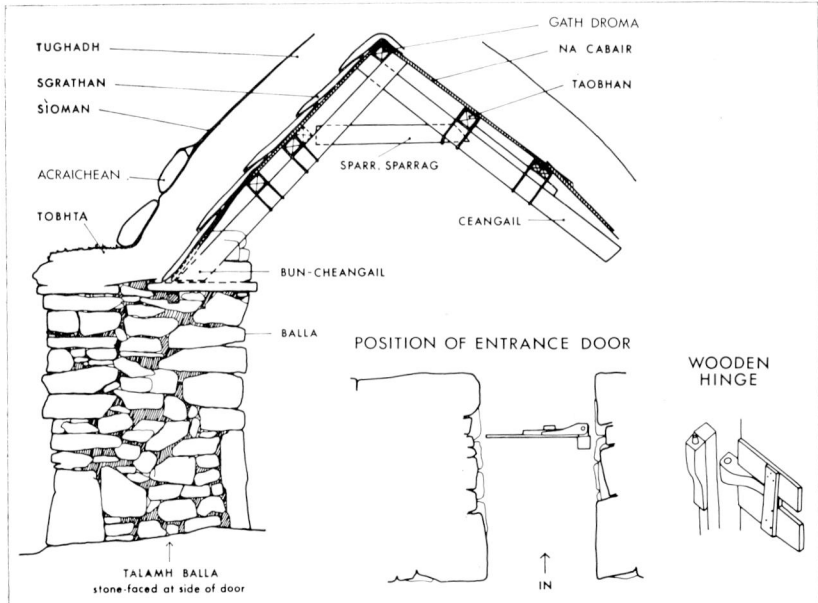

Fig. 5. Cross section through entrance, with details of door and wooden hinges. Gaelic terminology: *talamh balla*, hearting of wall; *tobhta*, wall-ledge; *acraichean*, anchor stones; *sìoman*, rope; *sgrathan*, turf; *tughadh*, thatch; *gath droma*, roof ridge; *na cabair*, roof timbers; *taobhan*, purlin; *sparr*, *sparrag*, tie beam; *ceangail*, couple; *bun-cheangail*, couple foot; *balla*, wall.

The chief difference between now and when the house was in full occupation is in the roofing timbers of the byre. The rafters then lay at a much more shallow angle. There were scarcely any tie beams, as a result of which the roof had sagged in a manner characteristic of the byre-ends of blackhouses in the area, since less care was taken in the construction of this part. [To counteract this, two upright poles were set in the middle of the floor, one actually springing from the byre drain. These have now been removed]. The byre roof has been raised to match the height of the house roof, and rafters with pegged and lashed tie-beams inserted throughout.

Another difference is in the living room and bedroom where the wallpaper has been removed. This formerly extended up the walls and a third of the way up the soot-blackened rafters of the roof of the living room. The bedroom was previously papered over the whole roof, and in order to make the roof take the paper, several planks and bits of boxes were nailed along the rafters, and across the hipped end.

These elements—roof-ridge, rafters, tie-beams, and purlins—are further strengthened and made rigid by coir yarn lashings at the crossings.

42 Arnol lies parallel to the road. The byre end was lower than the house end before the collapsing roof was reconstructed [1966].

Overlying the purlins are the vertical side-timbers, which [in the bedroom] include barrel staves and a tiller. These form a reasonably level surface for the overlying sods and thatch.

The timbers of the roof are covered with heathery sods, *sgrathan* [sing. *sgrath*], laid from eaves to ridge and overlapping like the scales of a fish. The ridge sods overlap on two sides. The thatch, formerly of bere-straw [now, as a rule of oat-straw], was laid from eaves to ridge in shaken-out bunches—without being drawn straight so that the straws lay parallel. It is fastened down by a fishing-net and by ropes, *siomain*, formerly of heather, now of coir-yarn. The ends of the ropes go round anchor stones, *acraichean*, about 25–30 cm long, lying about 30 cm up from the wall-head. Another row of stones, not fixed to the ropes, are set between these and the wall-head. The horizontal ropes tied or looped round the verticals as spacers are called *lùban* in the Arnol area.

At the apex of each hip, a protruding 'raven-stick', in Arnol the *maide fithich*, or *corra-thulchainn*, serves as an anchor for the ropes that hold the thatch on the hip.

42 Arnol after restoration. Note the squared-off corners of the walls. The heights of the house and byre roofs have been equalised [1968].

The hipped shape of the roof means that the underlying rafters have to be arranged in a particular way. A centre beam, *a' chorr* or *corra thulchainn* [whose extension upwards through the thatch is used as an anchor for the ropes] links the middle of the gable and the roof ridge. A pair of V-shaped members, *an roinn-oisinn*, stretch from each corner of the gable and side-walls to the roof-ridge. Since the first pair of rafters also meets here, there is a junction or overlapping of seven elements at the end of the roof-ridge.

There is no chimney or smoke-hole in the roof at 42 Arnol. This is a relic of the old tradition of allowing the thatch to become as much impregnated with soot as possible, for use as fertilizer in the fields [see pp. 35-36]. The only openings in the thatch are small, rectangular roof lights.

The end of the barn roof, showing ropes tied on to stones which keep the thatch in place and the stick which anchors the ropes at the hipped end [1973].

✥ WALLS, FLOORS AND HEARTH

The walls are of characteristic blackhouse form, with an inner and outer skin of stone, and a central core of peat-mould and earth. This core is the *uatabac*, also called the *talamh balla* or *glutaran* in other parts of Lewis. The rafters rest on the inner face of the wall, and the thatch comes down as far as the core. Water shed from the roof percolates through the core, helping to improve its insulating qualities in relation to both cold and wind. The outer part of the double wall remains open, forming a ledge, *tobhta*, on which it is easy to walk and from which the thatch can readily be replaced or repaired. The *tobhta* can be reached by a flight of steps, *staireachan*, here situated at the end of the byre. A thick layer of grassy sods on the ledge could make good eating for sheep. The width of the *tobhta* varies considerably, from about 46 cm at the end of the barn next to

The steps at the end of the byre, leading to the *tobhta* or wall ledge [1973].

the stackyard, to about 137 cm at the bedroom end of the house. The part that forms the gutter between the house and barn is 91 cm wide.

The bedroom and kitchen floors are roughly paved with flagstones. Linoleum was formerly laid in the bedroom.

The byre floor is of bare earth, whilst the barn floor is clayed at the point where threshing was done with the flail. The inner end of the barn floor is lined with substantial planks, on top of which the sheaves can be laid,

The kitchen, looking towards the byre. The walls and part of the roof were formerly papered [1966].

insulated from the damp of the floor. The outer part of the barn is flagged. This part has its own door, and is separated from the rest of the barn by a wooden partition.

In the centre of the kitchen floor is the central hearth, *cagailt*, using peat fuel, from the large stack at the back of the house. The iron links, *slabhraidh* [called 'strowlie' in Arnol], and the crook, *dubhan*, from which the pots and kettle are hung, are fastened to the roof-ridge, the strongest part of the roof-timbers.

The central hearth, with the crook and links above. On the left is the wooden settle or *being*. One of the three box beds opens into the kitchen [1966].

✣ LAYOUT AND FIXED FEATURES

The front door, *dorus*, opens on an entrance area, formerly used as the henhouse, called *stairseach* [threshold]. Both people and cattle had to use this entrance, but whereas in older blackhouses the door opened straight on to the byre, late nineteenth-century blackhouses are modified by the open area separating living room and byre.

To the left is the living room, *aig an teine* [at the fire], entered through a wooden partition which contains a half-door. The opening could be screened by a netting-wire frame to keep hens out. The kitchen leads on

The bedroom window is the only window in the house. It has two fixed panes [1966].

to the bedroom, *uachdar an tighe*. The partition, *tallan fiodha*, between kitchen and bedroom contains a wooden door with an iron sneck, and an opening giving access to a box-bed.

The bedroom is the only room with a wall window, *uinneag*, the opening for which has been cut through the top of the double wall. There are two rectangular panes in a wooden frame. The window does not open. All other windows in the house, byre and barn are fixed roof lights in the thickness of the thatch.

The byre is entered through a wooden partition to the right of the entrance door. It has stalls, *buabhall-na-bà*, along one side separated by three wooden partitions of a triangular shape. These are formed of vertical wooden planks nailed to an angled member that runs from the floor up to the base purlin. There are no troughs, and food for the cattle was simply laid into the forestall. The cattle were tied by ropes to an upright wooden pole fixed against the wall at the front of the stall. The floors of the stalls are raised slightly above the floor behind, where a drain leads the urine through a hole in the gable, *toll lodain*, to the field outside. There is a wooden loose-box for calves to the left of the byre door.

The unrestored byre with its sagging rafters supported by two wooden uprights [1966].

Fig. 6. *Buabhall-na-bà*, the byre stalls.

Formerly, it was the custom in blackhouses to let the manure accumulate in the byre throughout the winter. In spring, instead of removing it laboriously through the front door, the gable end was broken open. This opening was in some cases sealed with turf, and was called the *toll each*, 'horse hole', since this is where the cart or horse creels were loaded with dung. There is no evidence for such an opening at 42 Arnol, which again points to the relatively late building date, and the manure there was cleared out fairly regularly as it accumulated.

The barn, *sabhal*, lies in parallel with the house and byre, with its own roof, but sharing a common wall. It does not extend for the full length of the house and byre, however, and has in any case been shortened, as previously described. A door in the wall opposite the front door leads into it and in line there is a low, blocked up opening in the outer barn wall. This is the *toll fhasgnaidh*, or winnowing hole, set in line with the other doors to ensure a through draught for winnowing.

The top end of the barn is floored with wooden planks as a base for the sheaves. There is a roof light, *uinneag tughaidh*, in the hipped end here. When sheaves were required from the stackyard at the end of the house, it was the custom to open up the thatch around the window-opening and pitch the sheaves in there. In the middle section, the smooth clayed floor is adapted for the winnowing and flail threshing of the grain. The potatoes were also stored here, hence the name *cùil bhuntata* [potato

Fig. 7. *Toll fhasgnaidh* or winnowing hole.

The back of the barn. The blocked-up winnowing hole is to the right of the door [1966]

corner]. On the walls hung the flail, *sùist*, when not in use. It had three elements, a handstaff, *lorg*, a souple or beater, *buailtean*, [which was thicker and shorter than the handstaff] and a looped thong, *sail shùiste* [often of sheepskin] to link the other parts. The flail was swung over the shoulder or upper arm to beat out the grain from the ears of the sheaves. Winnowing with a shallow circular sieve or riddle, *criathar*, was afterwards necessary to get rid of the chaff and broken straw, before the grain was taken to the kiln to be dried for grinding. Sickles and scythes, spades, rakes, peat cutting irons, and other small hand tools were also to be found here, as

The end of the barn has a planked floor to take the sheaves, which could be pitched through the roof-opening in the hip [1966].

well as barrels and chests to hold food for the hens and animals. Fleeces from the annual wool clip were stored here, awaiting sale.

A wooden partition cuts off the outer part of the barn, which has its own exterior door. This section is the *cùil-nan-othaisgean*. Here if necessary, ewes could shelter at lambing time.

The outer and inner barn doors have wooden hinges, and the latch of the door between the barn and *stairseach* is opened by means of a peg and a length of string.

The other end of the barn has a clayed threshing floor; a potato-corner was later built against the wooden partition [1968].

❧ DRAINS

It is of interest to realise that considerable trouble was taken to make blackhouses dry. In addition to the byre-drain, which lies on the surface and is readily visible, there is also a system of drains below the flagstones of the floors. One drain runs right across the house and barn, through the front door, its course being marked by an irregular line of stones. Another main drain appears to run at right angles to this one, passing right underneath the central hearth. In wet weather, dampness from this drain can be seen rising in the sand in which the stones of the hearth are bedded.

This care in ensuring a dry house is not necessarily a late feature, since underfloor drains have a long history and are to be found even in the Neolithic houses at Skara Brae in Orkney.

❧ FURNISHINGS

There is nothing lavish about the furnishings of a blackhouse. Functionalism rather than ornament is the first consideration and furnishings tend to be substantially but plainly made of wood, painted or varnished a dark colour—usually brown. The best and most characteristic pieces are the dressers, the long wooden settles, and the box-beds. The typical dresser is open or has two cupboards below, two drawers above and a good working surface for jugs, bowls and other utensils. Behind this is a plate-rack, not necessarily attached to the dresser, whose top is angled to match the slope of the blackhouse roof. All the furniture is ranged along the sides of the walls, leaving as much working space as possible on the floor around the central hearth.

The bedroom at 42 Arnol has three box-beds, *leabaidh dhùinte*, one of which opens into the kitchen. They are curtained and have knitted covers [Fig. 8]. When the house was lived in there was a table, *bòrd*, with two leaves, a cupboard or *preas*, a chest, *ciste*, a dresser, *dreasar*, for clothes, and a clock, *uaireadair*, on the wall beside the window. A shelf above the door contained a variety of tins and odds and ends and attached to the wooden partition wall a Tilly-lamp, used before electricity was introduced. The floor was covered with linoleum.

The kitchen at present contains the basic blackhouse furnishings. The characteristic items are the dresser and plate-rack and the wooden settle, or *being*. Two drawers occupy half the length of the *being* and the other half, left open for storing articles such as footwear underneath, was curtained at the front.

At one end of the *being*, near the door for coolness, is a low cupboard that held the food supplies. Formerly there was a dresser for bed-covers and

Box-beds [right] in the bedroom, which formerly had linoleum on the floor. The walls were papered right across [1966].

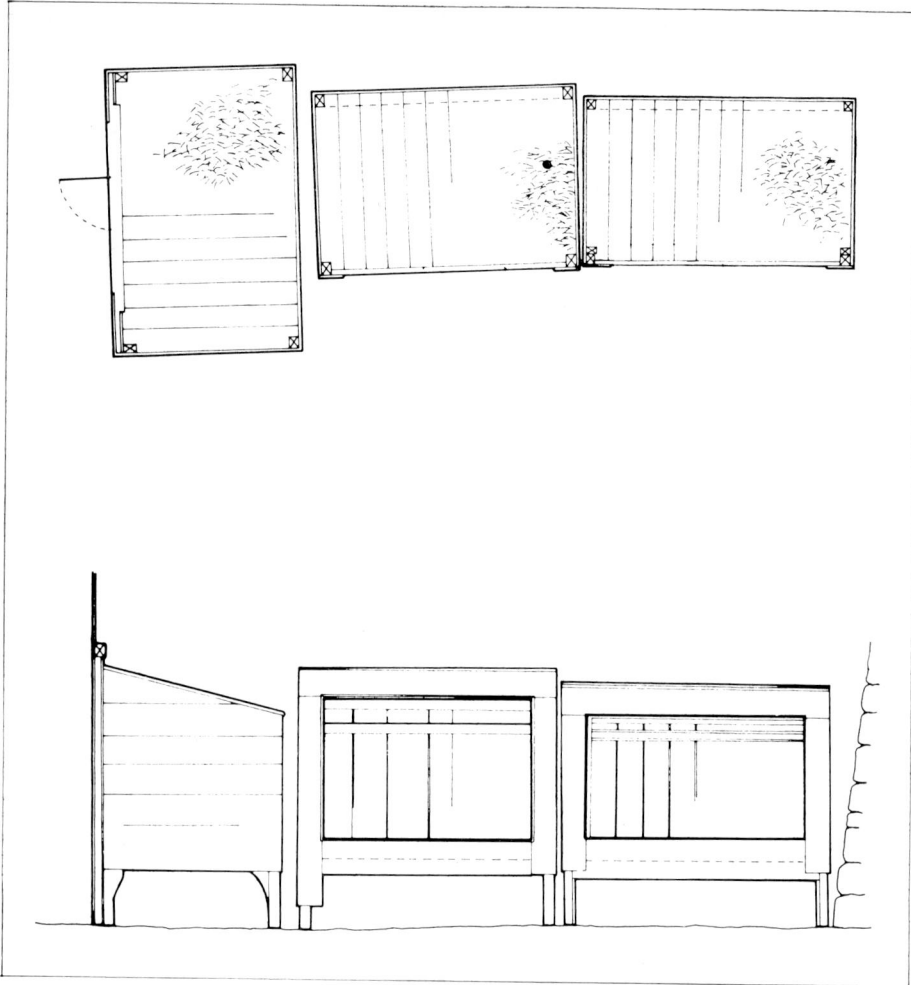

Fig. 8. Plan and section of the three box-beds in the bedroom. The one on the left opens on to the kitchen.

blankets at the other end of the *being*, beside the box-bed, and there was a square table nearby.

Along the opposite wall is a cupboard for crockery—a dresser with a well-shaped top and the unusual feature of two built-in mirrors and the traditional type of dresser and plate-rack. The dresser with mirrors is not local and in fact is a Lowland type, bought in Edinburgh shortly after the First World War. The same was true of a smaller, plainer, dresser, which formerly stood against this wall. The number of dressers in the house was unusual for a blackhouse.

Upright and rotary churns [1973].

A hanger made from a dried plant stem [1973].
The *lampa cheaird*, tinker's lamp, used in the byre during milking [1973].
Pendulum clock [1973].

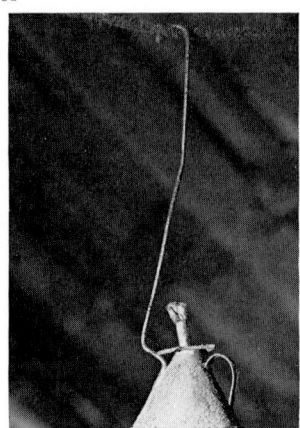

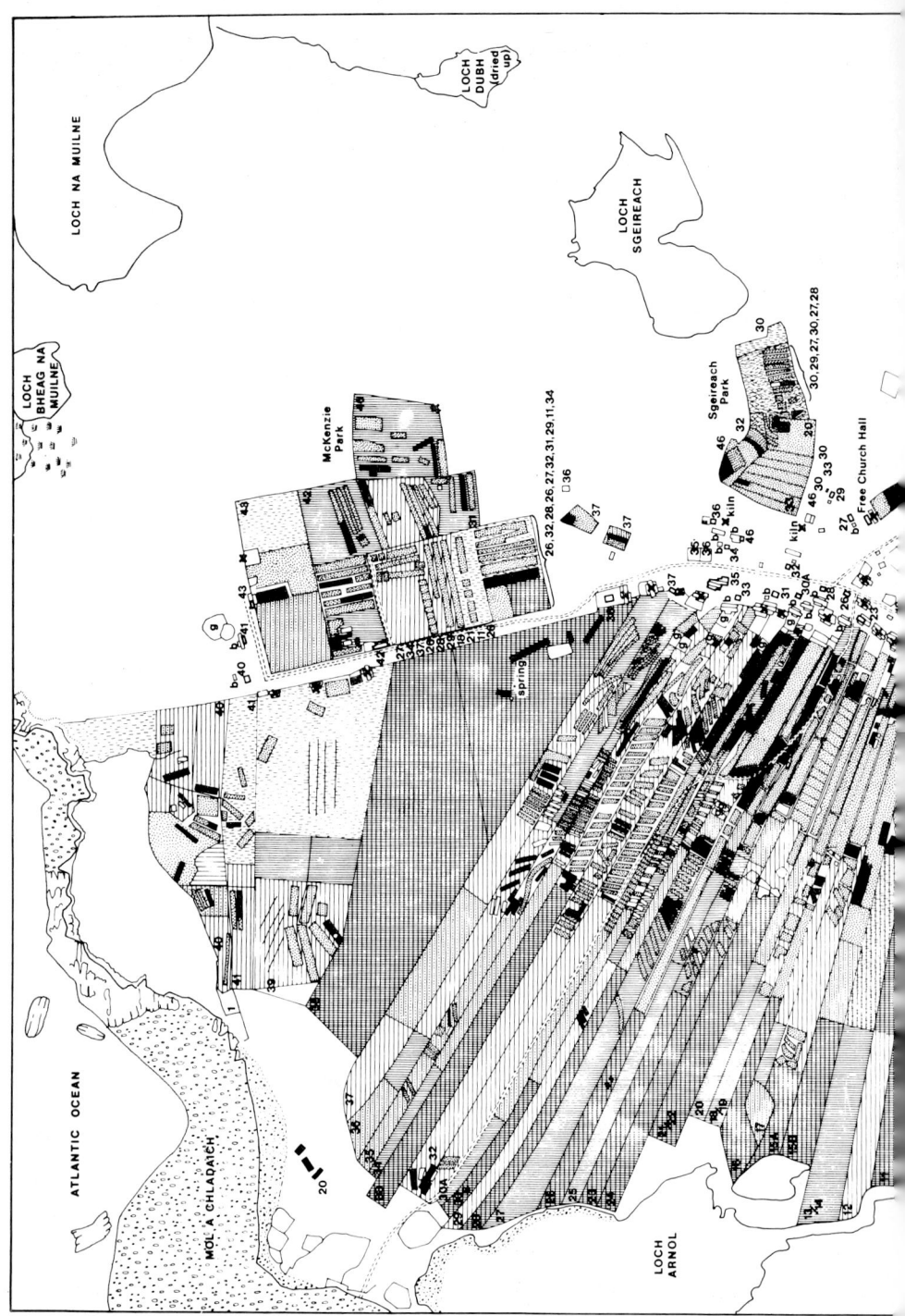

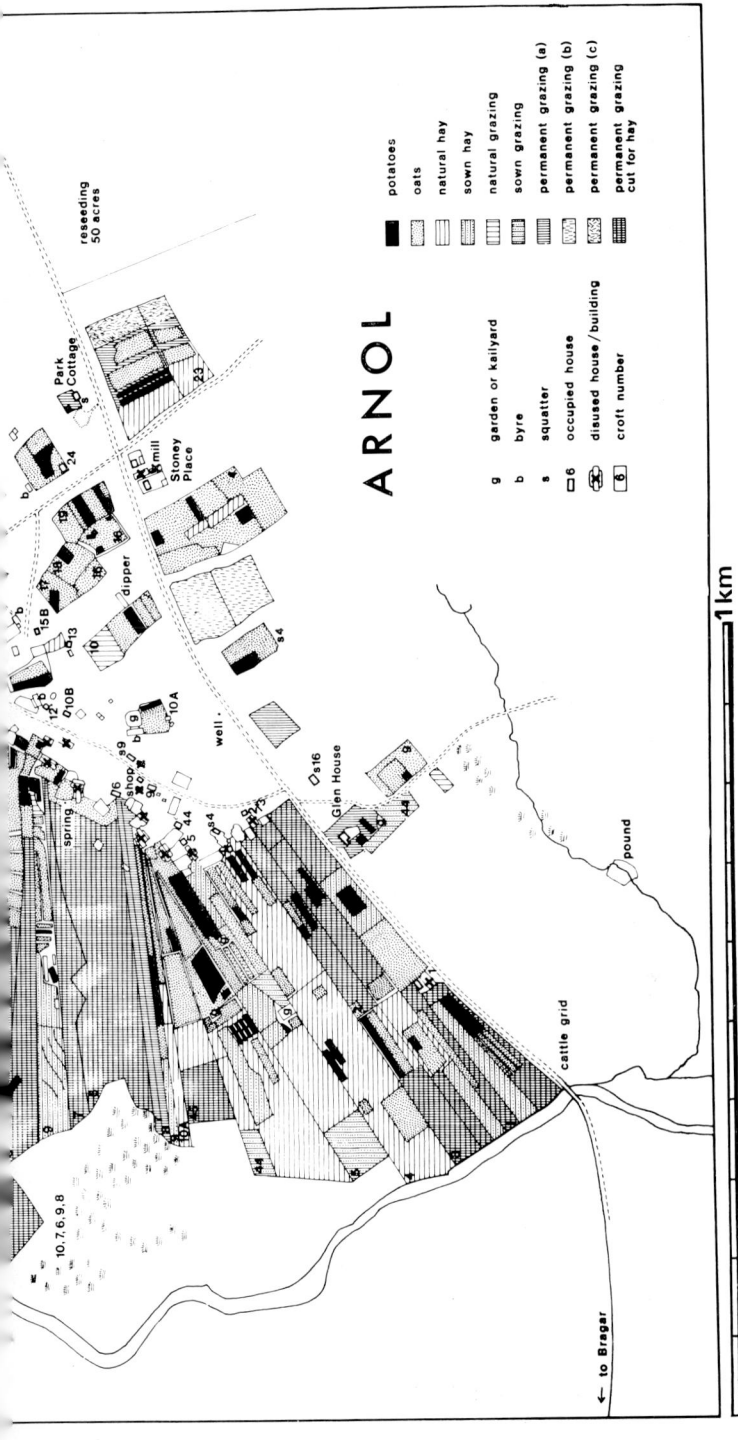

Fig. 9. Layout of the village of Arnol [based on a survey by the Department of Geography, University of Glasgow].

There is also a small chest, a stool, *stòl*, an iron girdle for baking, a tinker's lamp, *lampa cheaird*—often used in the byre during milking—an upright and a rotary churn, *cuinneag*, and a hanger, *cloran*, made of the dried and hardened stem and leaf-stalks of a kind of thistle that grows in sandy soil.

Another upright churn, without its lid and plunger, sits in the entrance area, alongside a crude table. The peats for the fire, brought in from the stack for convenience, are also stored in this area.

The terminology of the units and fixed features of the building is given in Fig. 3 [p. 10]; this may be compared with the layout of a century earlier [Fig. 10].

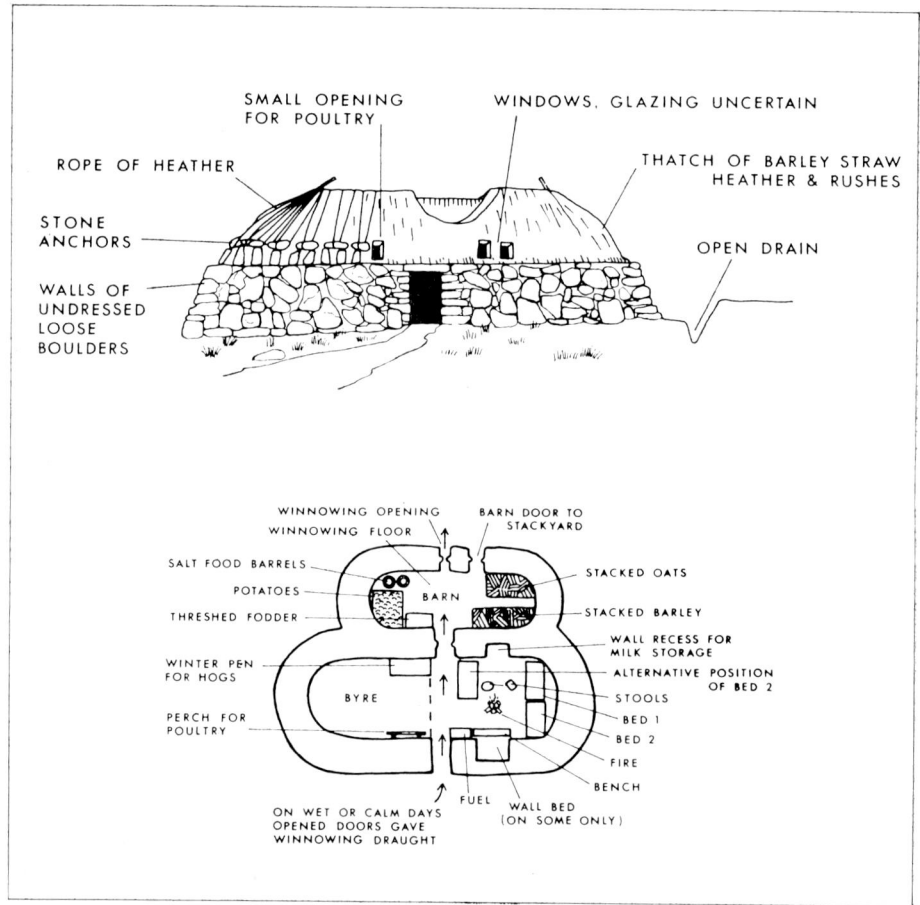

Fig. 10. Details of an Arnol blackhouse of pre-1870 type [adapted from drawings in *The West Side Story*, May, 1964, p. 23].

BLACKHOUSES ON THE WEST SIDE OF LEWIS

A question often asked is, 'what is the origin and meaning of the term "blackhouse" [*tigh dubh* in Gaelic]?' The word is not much more than a century and a half old. Until about 1850, all houses in Lewis, apart from castles, institutional buildings and associated dwellings, were of similar character. All had walls of double thickness, built of clay-mortared stone or drystone and turf, with thatched roofs. Since there were no others there was little need to use any name but 'house'. However, from the 1850s, new buildings of mainland type began to appear. Their single thickness walls, cemented with lime mortar, presented such a contrast that they got the name *tigh geal*, 'white house', and the antonym *tigh dubh* was then to be applied to the older houses in Lewis.

Nowadays, 'blackhouse' is often used loosely of any house in the Highlands and Islands with a thatched and, usually, hip-ended roof. It is preferable, however, to use it as a technical term for houses with walls of double thickness.

The very adoption of the name 'blackhouse' marked the beginning of the end of a long building tradition that goes back through the Middle Ages into the Viking period and beyond. 42 Arnol, built about 1875, is an excellent example of the transition, for though many of its features match those of earlier houses, others diverge from the older norms. Even though Lewis, and the West side in particular, has been more resistant to change than most other areas, nevertheless changing fashions and needs, changing social attitudes, estate and local authority regulations, and government legislation, have all had an effect, even on the blackhouse itself.

The strength of the tradition is emphasised more than anything else by the fact that blackhouses were being built in considerable numbers within the last 100 years. In fact, few surviving examples antedate the nineteenth century, though the ruins of older ones certainly can be found. From these, and from printed descriptions, it can be seen that even within this apparently rather inflexible building form, a good deal of variation was to be found, and a certain amount of change and adaptation was possible.

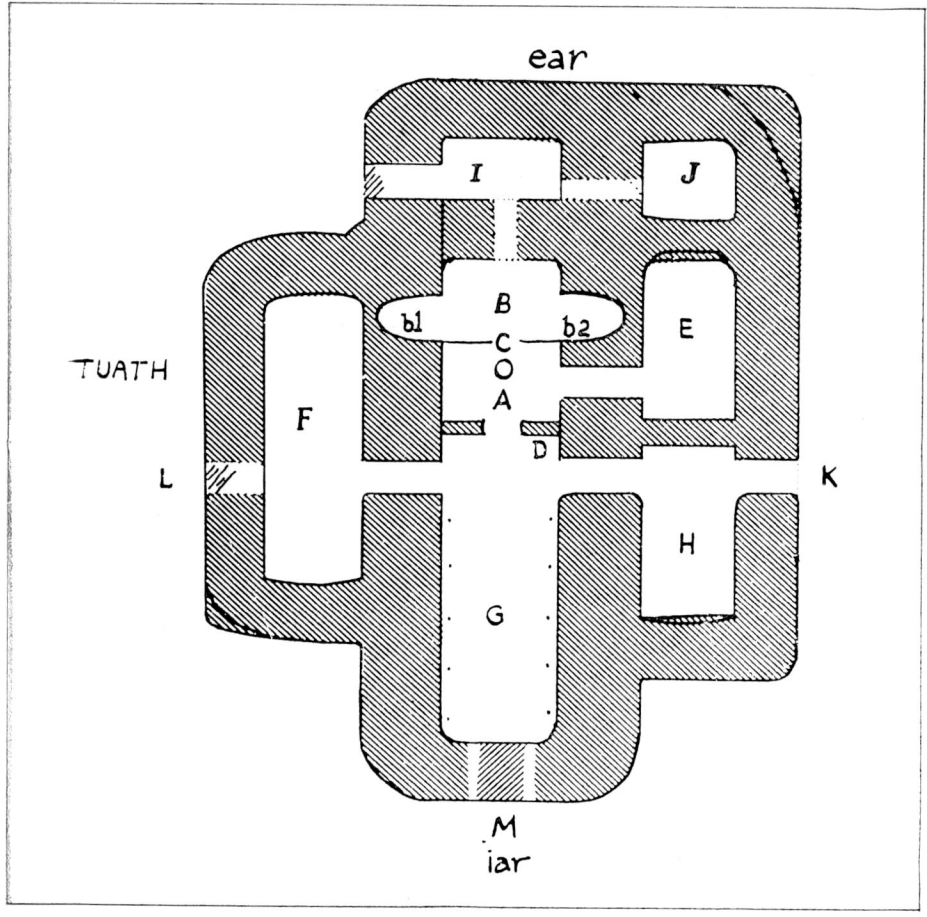

Fig. 11. Layout of an eighteenth-century blackhouse at Bragar [after *Gairm*, No. 32, 1962, p. 339]:
 [A] *aig an teine*, at the fire; [B] *cùlaist*, bedroom; [b1, b2 *crùb*], wall bed; [C] *cailbhe*, partition wall; [D] *tallan*, low partition; [E] *tigh uaraich*, closed room; [F] *sabhal*, barn; [G] *air an todhar*, byre; [G (dotted)] *stèill*, stake for cows; [H] *fosglan*, porch; [I] *àth*, kiln; [J] *tigh falaich*, hidden room (usable as a still) [K] *dorus beòil*, front door; [L] *toll an t-sabhail*, barn hole; [M] *toll each*, 'horse-hole', for byre manure; [O] *teine*, fire.

Without going into great detail, some of the main differences can be understood by contrasting the plan of an eighteenth-century blackhouse [no longer in existence] in the neighbouring village of Bragar with that of the nineteenth-century types. Broadly speaking, the more recent examples of the type of 42 Arnol are regularised and simplified forms of an older type characterised by a greater agglomeration of units, often falling into three lines in parallel, and generally with one single entrance. The core of the blackhouse at all periods is the conjoint, freely intercommunicating byre and dwelling-house. In earlier examples, entrance to the house was through the byre. The outer skin of the walls of this central unit supported the roofs of the secondary units. In some cases, the roof of one section of a unit might be put on at right angles to the rest.

The parallel units rarely coincide in length. The front unit was the entrance area, the *fosglan*, with space for the hand mill that ground the grain for everyday use, and an area for storage or for temporary use as a stable in bad weather. It is usually quite short, though the Bragar blackhouse has additional sections that make the front unit almost as long as the central one.

The inner door, exactly opposite the front door, opens into the byre for the cattle, which were tethered to upright wooden stakes. There was a low partition of stone or turf between the animals and the dwelling area. In later times this became a gable or roof-height partition, usually of wood, with a door in it. A further development was the separation of the sleeping-end from the living-room area by a similar partition. This feature is shown in the Bragar house diagram, but probably is not original. In the sleeping-end two beds are shown in the thickness of the wall, running straight in. In other old blackhouses, such wall beds run parallel to the wall, with a small front opening for access. These beds were rarely built into nineteenth-century blackhouses and in any case they began to go out of use after about 1850, when closed wooden box-beds began to come into fashion.

A third door immediately opposite the other two, leads into the third unit, the barn, where the cereal crops were stored and threshed with the flail on a clay floor. In order to get a draught for the subsequent winnowing, there was a low opening in the rear of the barn wall, in line with the three doors. When all stood open, there was an adequate through-draught for blowing the light chaff to one side as the grain trickled from a container on to a sheet on the floor.

The extra rooms in the Bragar blackhouse served several purposes. The largest, *an tigh uaraich*, had a door opening into the fire-room, but was closed off from the entrance area. It provided extra sleeping accommodation and storage for clothes, meal, salt meat, and sometimes milk and dairy produce.

The remaining two small chambers are said to be a corn-drying kiln and a place where illicit whisky was distilled.

Features like the last two, as well as the wall-beds, and the entrance porch or *fosglan*, disappeared from nineteenth-century blackhouses, and a conjoint byre and house, with a barn in parallel at the back, became the norm. The porch was often replaced by an open area between the byre and the living-end, as at 42 Arnol, which could be used as a kind of scullery. The outer and inner doors remained in line with the winnowing hole, but an extra barn door was usually added. This gave access to part of the barn for horses in bad weather, or for ewes and lambs. The original functions of the entrance porch were split up in this way between the area between byre and living-room, and the barn.

Another nineteenth-century feature in Lewis blackhouses was that the walls were all of stone, apart from the earth infilling of the core. They were not always like this. To judge by the comments of the officers of the Ordnance Survey in 1849–52, most blackhouse walls were built of a combination of sods and stones, often of peat sods lined internally with stones. The later buildings, therefore, were constructed in a more enduring manner than their predecessors. This also explains why relatively few early examples of blackhouses survive.

The dresser and plate-rack are standard pieces of furniture [1973].

CHANGE AND CONSERVATISM

Buildings like 42 Arnol are admirable examples of both change and conservatism in vernacular architecture. They look backwards as well as forwards in time, showing both the effects of, and resistance to, imposed changes. From as early as the 1830s, Lord Seaforth was telling his tenants to erect a partition between themselves and the cattle, and saying that 'more light should be admitted into the dark recesses of their habitations'. He succeeded in effecting some reforms, but 'sorely against the wishes of the people'.

In 1872 in the township of Barvas, crofters were made to improve their houses by putting in two doors and making a division between house and byre, the proprietor himself supplying doors, windows, and woodwork [*Evidence*, 1884, Appx. A, XLI, pp. 157–174].

In spite of efforts by landlords at improvement, it could still be said in a *Confidential Report to the Secretary for Scotland on the Condition of the Western Highlands and Islands*, in October 1886, that the 'houses in Lewis are generally of an inferior description, mainly because of the obstinate retention of cattle under the roof... and of the inveterate custom of annually transferring to the land, as manure, the entire thatch of the dwelling. This latter custom rests on the belief that thatch saturated with peat-smoke is a valuable fertiliser, and, accordingly, no thin layer of turf is interposed, as usual in the Highlands, between the rafters and the straw covering. To provide an exit for smoke would also be thought, for the same reason, a wasteful proceeding: and it is thus allowed to find its way through the roof wherever chinks exist. This also in contravention of the conditions on which the lands are held, but it is hopeless for any proprietor to attempt, single-handed, to control masses of disaffected people such as must be dealt with here' [*Confidential Report*, 1886, p. 16].

For the nineteenth century, especially after the surveying and re-allotting of crofting land in 1849, '50, '51, till about roughly the period when 42 Arnol was built and when the Estate began to offer improving leases, the features of the Lewis blackhouse may be summarised as follows:

Oblong in shape, often with rounded corners on the older houses, varying in length and width but averaging 6·1 m wide externally and usually between 9·14–18·29 m in length. This gives an internal size of 3·7–4·3 m by 6·1–7·6 m long.

Double-skin walls with an earthen core, about 1·5–1·8 m high, by 1·5 m or more wide. Later examples at least were built with an external batter that gave a top wall width of about 1·1 m.

A single entrance-door for men and cattle, often no windows, and no chimney. Any roof light had a pane of skin or glass, as much to retain the smoke as to keep out the weather.

Rafters springing from the top of the inner skin of the wall, with purlins overlain by vertical cabers or branches to support the divots and straw thatch. Roofs often let in rain, wet drops of tarry soot fell freely on occasion, and walls were often damp inside.

Annual stripping of thatch for use as manure. This practice affected the grazing in some areas, for fresh divots had to be cut each year from the areas of grassy heath, and divots for even a single house could strip a considerable area of ground. Fresh thatch, of bere-straw rather than heather if it was to be used as manure, was also required each year.

Hipped roofs, whose shape enhanced wind resistance, and ropes of hand-twisted heather looped round anchor stones just above the eaves, to keep the straw in place.

The byre, occupying roughly two-thirds of the main room, with wall-stakes to which the cattle were tied.

The barn, generally built at the back of the house [more rarely at right angles to one end], accessible from the main room but originally with no external door. There was usually a winnowing hole, to allow a draught for winnowing grain.

An entrance passage or room that opened into the byre end, usually having a shelf for the hand-quern, and if big enough serving as a temporary winter stable for the horse.

Sometimes an additional room, the 'locked-end', accessible from the fire-room, used for sleeping and storage.

Neuk beds in the thickness of the wall, lying either parallel or at right angles to the wall, usually at the side of the fire but sometimes also in the barn. From about 1850 wooden box-beds with closing fronts were replacing the neuk-beds.

The removal of dung from the byre once a year only, in spring. In May, when a visitor entered a blackhouse, he might step 30 cm down into the empty byre, then up again into the living area. The levels were gradually equated by dung and added earth and seaweed, and towards spring it was mounded high, ready to be removed again in creels on the human back or on horse-back, or in carts. The gable end of the byre wall could be broken out to facilitate the emptying of the byre and the temporary nature of this gable, *toll each*, can still be observed on many surviving blackhouses.

The erection of a new building against an old one when a member of the family hived off and got married.

A central hearth on flagstones at floor level [one still occupied in 1964 had the bed-stone of a horizontal mill as the base for the fire]. A seat or bench, often of turf, was alongside, later replaced by a wooden settle, *séiseach*, chests also served as seats, and stools. Men and women tended to sit at different sides of the hearth.

These general characteristics started to undergo more rapid modification after 1879. The improving leases offered by the Estate after that date insisted that houses had to have at least two apartments. This meant that the practice of cutting off the bedroom, *cùlaisd*, from the kitchen by means of a wooden partition and door became general. Rule 48 of the Estate Regulations, in fact, insisted on separate sleeping apartments for single men and women [*Report*, 1902, pp. lxxxv–lxxxvi]. The byre was also required to be separate, thatch was not to be stripped annually for manure, and the cattle dung was to be cleared regularly to an outside dung-hill, not left to accumulate till spring. The 1879 Rules and Regulations of the Lewis Estate are specific:

'The dwelling-houses to be erected by the tenants . . . shall be of stone and lime, or of stone and clay pinned and harled with lime, or with stone on the outer face, and turf or sod on the inside, and roofed with slates, tiles, or straw, or heather with divots . . . each house to have at least two apartments, with a glazed window in the wall of each, and a closet or small room, with chimneys in the gables, or other opening for smoke in the roof; the thatch or covering not to be stripped off or removed for manure; the byre to be built at the end of the back of the dwelling-house, as the site may admit, and to have a separate entrance. In the byre a gutter to be formed for manure, which shall be regularly removed to a dung heap outside' [*Report*, 1902, Appx. H, p. 38].

On 11 February 1893, the Lewis District Committee minuted a regulation involving complete separation of byre and dwelling end by a wall, with no internal communication, and the Sanitary Inspector was instructed to institute legal proceedings where necessary. But though some cases were tried, new houses were nevertheless being built on the old pattern in 1898 and no doubt later [*Report*, 1902, p. lxxxviii, p. xc]. Indeed as recently as 1947, about 40% of the Lewis homesteads still had house and byre intercommunicating under one roof [Geddes, 1955, p. 79].

Another factor that affected building patterns in the late nineteenth century was the programme of construction of roads and footpaths undertaken under the Western Highlands and Islands Act of 1891–7. In 1893–4, for example, Arnol had 731 m of road constructed, 3·4 m wide, and in 1896–7, a further 1,033 m, 2·7 m wide. Here and in other Lewis villages [and generally in the Highland areas], roads had a magnetic effect that drew the houses to their sides, ultimately giving the villages a characteristically linear layout.

But in spite of both Estate and County Council regulations, the blackhouse tradition persisted with a tenacity that brought places like 42 Arnol right through almost to the present day as lived-in, functioning units that retained much of the old style, albeit with modifications. Thus at 42 Arnol, house and byre are still under one roof, communicating internally though separated by an entrance chamber that in older houses would have formed part of the byre. The barn is in parallel at the back, but it has a door of its own in addition to a low opening, the winnowing hole. There are several roof lights in the thatch and a wall window has been knocked out in the bedroom, which is separated from the fireroom by a partition and door. Sleeping accommodation consists of three box beds.

The walling itself also shows some modification, for it is pretty well squared off at the corners, and the stones are fairly even in size, partly squared and laid in courses.

The roof is hipped at each end and the thatch is held down against the wind by ropes and anchor stones that form a double row around the foot of the thatch.

The road runs hard by the front wall.

42 Arnol, therefore, though less than a hundred years old, admirably typifies the nature of both the change and conservatism that characterised the West side and other parts of Lewis until relatively recent times—indeed until Government grants for house improvements became readily available.

THE VILLAGE OF ARNOL

Arnol is a village or township situated at the south-west corner of the parish of Barvas. It lies to the seaward side of the A 858 road, on land owned by the Barvas Estate Ltd.

Arnol has a long history as a settlement cluster, though the houses have not always been in their present positions. The original site was much nearer the sea, in the area above the rocky beach called Mol a' Chladaich, immediately to the north of Loch Arnol. Here the ruins of small, oval-ended stone houses are still visible. No doubt they date from and beyond the eighteenth century. They lie on an accumulation of layers of sand, varying in depth, in which successive occupation layers are marked by pottery going back at least to the 1st century A.D. On this site, there was easy access to the resources in fish and fowl of the sea and the loch. In the hollow behind the little settlement lay the community's fields, still outlined by stone or built up on their lower edges to make level beds or platforms. A large rounded stone, prominent from its white colour, was used by the young lads as a trial for their growing strength. The stock of sheep and cattle, horses—and perhaps at one time, goats—grazed on the slopes above of Cnoc a' Charnain, Cnoc na Glas Bhuaile, Knock More Arnol, and beyond.

It was a good site in summer. But when the winter storms swept in, it was exposed, liable in part to erosion and in part liable to be overwhelmed by the heaping up of beach boulders. This accumulation also made it difficult to drain the boggy area in the hollow behind the houses. Here, no doubt, was the source of peat for fuel, gradually used up through the centuries. Shortage of fuel in the immediate vicinity, increasing difficulties due to the nature of the coast, and an expanding population in the eighteenth century were amongst the main factors that led to re-siting of the village in its present position, a little farther inland. Similar moves from sites hard by the shore were made by other Lewis villages, such as Shawbost, and in this Arnol conforms to an eighteenth-century pattern.

For Arnol, the move away from the sea did not matter greatly. There is no harbour, though before the 1914–18 war it was possible for boats to lie at anchor at Port Arnol, from April till October. From the early 1920s, sea-erosion and silting made the anchorage unusable. Small boats, however, can lie in hollows among the stones of the foreshore, among the old, half-eroded fields and houses, though considerable labour is involved in hauling them up from the sea. Boats and fishing, therefore, play only a small part in Arnol's existence, except for a few fish for home supply, some of them caught by fishing with limpet-baited lines from the rocks of Eilean Arnol. It is clear that the lack of a sea-outlet was felt by the inhabitants, for in 1889 they made representations for a boatslip to the Commission appointed to enquire into *Certain Matters Affecting the Interests of the Population of the Western Highlands and Islands of Scotland*, but with no good result.

There is little recorded history about Arnol in its past or present positions. According to an officer of the Ordnance Survey who was working in the area in 1848, it was 'a small village of miserably made huts, they are built of stone and peat sods and thatched with straw and heather'.

To the north-east of Arnol, place names reflect something of the earlier functionalism of village life, in particular the two lochs with the same name, Loch na Muilne, 'mill loch'. The stream that flowed from these, debouching in the sea at the Geodha Leathainn, at one time turned four or five little mills. South-west of Arnol, the stream, Allt na Muilne, flowing into Loch Arnol suggests the site of another mill for grinding grain. The last mill to be used by the Arnol crofters, in the early years of this present century, can still be seen on the stream flowing out of Loch Urahag, to the north of the road bridge that carries the A 858 over it. Though roofless, the walls still stand in part and the area for housing the water wheel can be seen. The site of the mill-lade is clearly visible. Though the grinding of grain had to go on into the darkness when necessary, this was not considered a canny place to be in at night.

The present-day croft land of Arnol slopes fairly steeply from the narrow flat sandy machair area to the present road near which the houses are sited. Beyond this the land levels out at about the 30·5 m contour to a thinly covered peat moor from which the peat must have been removed over a long period. Now the Arnol peat banks lie well to the north, beyond the two lochs called Loch na Muilne.

Agriculture is impeded by hummocky, stony outcrops and glacial boulders and debris. Loose stones, however, have been useful for building dykes, for example to enclose pieces of land on the common grazing. The soil is everywhere poor and hard to work because of stones. The pattern was little different in the eighteenth century, when Barvas parish generally was described as having 'light, thin, spouty ground, and in many places so full of stones, that the plough cannot go through it'. The best soil, on the machair, is no longer cultivated, but is used to grow hay.

The land of the crofts aligned from the road to the machair has a generally radial appearance because the strips widen at the shore. They range in size from half-crofts of 0·6 ha to a full croft of over 6·1 ha. 42 Arnol, at 1·9 ha, lies close to the average size of 2 ha. The 6·1 ha croft is exceptionally large because it acquired extra land when the present boundaries were set out in 1880.

Almost every crofter, however, has in addition other pieces of land which he cultivates or grazes. McKenzie Park, for instance, a dyke enclosed area on the common grazings, is shared between a dozen different crofts, including 42 Arnol. Sgeirach Park is similarly shared between eleven crofters, and the machair land and the land alongside the stream running into Loch Arnol is also split up for grazing. Some crofters also have dyke enclosed areas on the common grazing or immediately behind their houses. Any single croft, therefore, may have the use of a number of individual pieces of land, which can add considerably to its official area. Subletting of a croft, usually to another member of the family, may also take place.

The stackyard and other dykes around 42 Arnol [1973].

Apart from the areas enclosed by stone dykes there was no fencing until relatively recently, but the availability of Government grants had led to the fencing of all crofts except two by 1960. Like the thatched blackhouses alongside the modern buildings, the stob and wire fences alongside dykes of stone and turf give a sense of looking two ways in time. Here, as in other villages, the new fences make movement across the fields a matter of some difficulty.

Before 1880, the village consisted of a few crofts on the machair, of which the ruins survive on the foreshore. When the village moved to the road, it was still blackhouses that were erected at first. At the same time, however, a number of houses were put up by squatters on the common grazing, leading to a slightly ragged pattern of settlement, apart from the more regular roadside crofts. According to evidence given in 1884 by Norman Campbell, crofter in Arnol, to *Her Majesty's Commission of Inquiry into the Condition of the Crofters and Cottars in the Highlands and Islands of Scotland*, the number of families in the village had increased from nineteen to forty-five who paid rent, with ten more who had no land. This increase was said to be the natural increase of the people, only one or two families having come in from outside.

There were no restrictions on the siting of houses, least of all for the squatters on the common grazings. In evidence given to the Commission of Inquiry, the story was told of one man who went with his rent to Stornoway, having missed rent-collection day, and found the rent of the croft had already been paid by a new tenant. 'The new entrant built a house right in front of the old man's door so that he could scarcely enter it with a creel of peats on his back.'

Nine blackhouses were still occupied in Arnol in 1960, but only one, No. 42, retained the central hearth.

THE ECONOMIC PATTERN

Because of the difficult nature of the terrain, cultivation first required the removal of stones into clearance heaps or consumption dykes, and then the thin soil was scraped together into rigs or beds, called *feannagan*, to concentrate it in small areas. These beds were cultivated by the spade, an instrument that was coming into wider use from about the 1840s. At that time, it was said, 'a little refinement of taste, more than a sense of its disadvantages has in some instances abolished the use of the crooked spade, a very indelicate tool for females; for which the common spade is now substituted'. The 'crooked spade' or *caschrom* is at the present day unknown as a working tool in the West side of Lewis. It is in fact likely that the East coast fishing, which took the men away from home for long periods and left the women to see to much of the farm work, hastened the early replacement of the *caschrom* by the spade, for the *caschrom* is normally regarded as a man's tool.

In Arnol, one man used a hand-tractor in 1960, and another had a half share in a horse. An ordinary tractor was used only in helping to cut some of the hay and in that case was hired from another crofting township.

Formerly, there was much more intensive cultivation, and traces of old cultivation beds show that some of the hill common was once under the spade.

The present day crops are oats, potatoes and hay, the latter both sown and natural, and some patches of turnips. Some cabbages are grown. No particular rotation appears to be kept. 42 Arnol, whose 1·9 ha were worked by the family themselves, used to grow about 0·4 ha of oats, 0·3 ha of potatoes, and 0·08 ha of turnips, using as manure shell-sand and artificial fertilisers. The ground was worked by hiring or borrowing a tractor.

Oats are cut by the scythe or reaper, in former days by the sickle, *corran*, and bound by hand on the knee, by means of straw bands, into sheaves, each of which contains little more than two good handfuls of straw. They are then set up in stooks, *adagan,* and left to dry in the fields before being taken home to be built into small, circular stacks, *cruachan,* in the dyke-enclosed yard at the back of the house—adjacent to the barn where the crop had to be thrashed by the flail to separate ears and straw. At 42 Arnol, the thatch around the window in the hip-end of the barn roof was opened up to allow the sheaves from the stacks to be thrown in easily.

In earlier times bere [an old form of barley] was also grown, since it was bere straw that was used for thatching in the days when thatch was taken from the roofs each year for manure. Bere gave a higher yield of meal than oats, but bere-meal fell out of favour quickly after imported wheat flour became readily available.

After the harvest had been safely gathered, the work of processing it for food began. The first stage was to thrash it in the barn, using the flail, *sùist.* In earlier times the ears were often rubbed off the bere-stalks by using the feet, a method known as *a' suathadh an eòrna,* so that the straw should not be broken and could then be used for thatching the houses. Next the grain was winnowed to clear away the chaff and empty husks, and then the ears were dried in preparation for grinding. Where a quern or hand-mill stood by the entrance door of the blackhouse, small quantities of grain could be dried, prior to grinding, over the fire in a pot [or sometimes in a net, called a *tarran* in Uist].

For work on a bigger scale the stone-built corn-drying kiln, *àth,* was used. There were at least four of these in Arnol. They were separate buildings with one straight and one rounded gable. The single door was in a side wall near the straight gable, and the kiln itself was built into the rounded end. Essentially, an Arnol kiln consisted of a raised platform of stone standing about 76 cm high containing the bowl or *surrag* about 91–107 cm in diameter, with a flue called the *cailleach* or *cailleach na h-àthain* extending about 1·8–3 m out along the side of the barn wall. The fire of hard, dry peats was lit at the open end of the flue, which carried the heat into the bowl, under the drying floor. The drying floor itself consisted of wooden spars laid across the top of the bowl like the spokes of a wheel, joining in the middle to form a shallow cone. This arrangement appears to be peculiar to Arnol, since in most other places the spars lay flat. Over the spars, straw drawn straight out was laid deep enough to form a bed for the grain, which was laid about 30 cm deep on it. Three large bags of grain could be dried at a time, in 6–8 hours, with three dryings a day at the busy period when everyone was eager to get the first corn of the season dried and ground into fresh meal. The grain had to be turned regularly by hand to achieve even drying, and when the time came the *bodach,* the man in charge, would test it with his teeth. If ready, it was spread over the clay floor of the barn and beaten by one or two men with flails to remove the husks. Earlier on it was rubbed with the feet for the same purpose, the feet being scuffled from side to side, using the heel as the point of rotation.

One drying was called a *tireadh*, and a good *tireadh* could yield two bags of oatmeal.

Once dried, the grain was taken for grinding to the mill: the last which survived in use has been described above. The earlier and much smaller

The last horizontal mill to be used at Arnol; by 1928 it was grinding only barley: *photograph H. L. Dougal.*

type of mill had a horizontally turning water-wheel linked directly to the upper grind-stone, without gearing. Because of the position of the water-wheel, these are often technically called 'horizontal mills'. Water from the lade was concentrated by means of a narrow chute on the blades of the wheel, which turned below the floor of the mill in a lower chamber. Inside the mill, a wooden hopper was suspended above the mill-stones. The grain was filled into the hopper and trickled out of it into a wooden shoe which directed it into the eye of the upper mill-stone to be ground into meal. Vibrations communicated to the hopper by a stick that rubbed on the turning mill-stone helped to ensure a regular flow. Crofters used

Interior of a horizontal mill at Bragar, showing the machinery characteristic of Lewis—early twentieth century.

these mills once or twice a year, several families sometimes sharing one mill, and it was said that enough grain could be ground in 48 hours to last a family for the whole year. The problem was not the grinding, granted a plentiful supply of water, but the difficulty of getting enough grain dried and dehusked in advance for grinding. Following this, the meal was put through a sieve, *criathar*, to get rid of the fragments of husk.

The potato crop was and is taken up by a method that is almost, though not quite, localised in Lewis. This involves a smithy made instrument called a *croman*, a kind of adze-shaped mattock with a short wooden handle about 76 cm long. The worker moves along the drill, picking out each stem and spreading the tubers with the *croman* blade before gathering them into a pail which, when full, is emptied into a sack or creel. *Croman* blades, formerly hand-forged from sections of cart-wheel rings, are now shaped from sheet-steel by an oxy-acetylene cutter in the smithy in Stornoway.

Hay is cut in the same way as the cereal crop, dried in the field in small, circular hay-cocks, and finally brought to the yard and built into stacks of a rectangular shape, to which the Gaelic name *sig* is given.

For manuring the crops, the fertilisers in current use are the concentrated chemical compounds supplied by agricultural merchants. Shell-sand is used as a source of lime, but a formerly common manure, seaweed, was in 1960 being used by only one crofter, who carried it in traditional fashion in a creel on his back from the shore. Byre manure is also applied, but the use of soot-impregnated thatch has long since ceased.

About half the Arnol crofts have kitchen gardens in the enclosed yards behind the houses, where cabbage, carrots, and sometimes lettuce are grown.

A harvest of another kind was that of peat, to provide winter fuel for the fire. The Arnol peat-banks lie about 1·6–3·2 km away, and the peats are now taken home by tractor and bogey, but formerly by horses and carts or in creels on horseback.

Peat is one natural resource that exists in great plenty in Lewis, but constant peat-cutting over the centuries has had the effect of continually moving the banks away from the townships, so that greater distances have to be travelled to get to the peat, with corresponding increases in time spent and in expense. A compensating factor, however, is that the clearance of peat exposed the underlying mineral soils, which eventually could be reclaimed for grazing or cropping.

It is a remarkable sight to visit Arnol about October, when the peats are home and stacked by the houses, their dark bulk almost dwarfing the buildings themselves.

In statistical terms, a crofting household of four persons, burning nothing but peat, would use approximately 15,000 peats in a year. A good man working the peat-spade, *taraisgear*, in the peat bank, could cast 1000 a day, so that he had to spend a minimum of 15 days, given continuous good weather, at this job. Later the peats had to be set up to dry, they had to be transported, and they had to be stacked at home. It is estimated that peat work occupied about a month of the crofter's year, and unless a good surplus of labour was available, this could seriously interfere with the working of the croft. In practice, neighbours and relatives work at the job together and the various processes are done with expedition and also with enjoyment of a communal task. Apart from coal, which due to freight charges is expensive, there is no alternative to peat in the almost treeless island of Lewis.

The stock carried on the Arnol crofts averages one cow and its calf, and about twenty to seventy sheep. In 1960 there were considerable losses in sheep due to disease in the lambs and also to the ravages of buzzards and an eagle. At this level and in such circumstances there is very little margin of difference between profit and loss.

During the summer months the sheep are gathered at the fanks [sheep-folds] four times, for shearing and marking, castration, weaning and dipping, in addition to the gatherings for lambing in April and for tupping in Autumn.

The sale of wool and wethers [castrated rams] is the crofters' main source of income. Calves are also sold, and with re-seeding the wether lambs are grazed on the re-seeded areas and sold the same autumn, at about six months old.

The amount of byre accommodation in the blackhouses, and the small number of cattle kept now by individual crofters, is eloquent testimony to the changes in emphasis that have been taking place in the latter half of the nineteenth and in the twentieth century.

Sheep and cattle have exchanged places in importance, and this is a change that is far more fundamental and far-reaching than might appear at first sight, for it marks more than anything else the end of the older traditional way of life. When cattle played the chief part in the economy, the system of transhumance—the annual movement of cows, calves and people, along with the formerly much smaller stock of sheep, to the summer shielings—was an integral part of the annual cycle of subsistence and survival. But in the course of the nineteenth century sheep came to absorb the hill grazings more and more and the use of summer shielings gradually died out, though continuing longer in Lewis than in any other part of Britain.

In 1848–52 the Ordnance Survey Name Books recorded numerous shielings of stone and turf, or of turf alone, occupied in summer for about six weeks, and most often marked in place-names by the element *airidh*.

The shielings were normally congregated in more or less scattered groups, depending on the nature and extent of the grazing and the Name Books indicate that as a rule, many of these were in ruins and relatively few were in regular seasonal occupation by the mid-nineteenth century. The system was already breaking down, though shielings remained quite common till 1939, and in 1960 one Arnol man spent the summer at his shieling of stone and turf, with his two cows. The great majority of Lewis crofters over middle age have personal knowledge of shieling life.

Whilst the stock, the women and the young folk were at the shieling, the young crops were growing unmolested in the unfenced fields and cultivation beds around the villages and there was relatively little disturbance in unroofing the houses to use the thatch as manure. In any case, as often as not in the nineteenth century, the men went off at shieling time, to the East coast fishing.

With the loss of the hill pastures to sheep, some form of compensation has been necessary in spite of the reduced numbers of cattle, and accordingly reseeding of 36 ha of hill pasture for improved grazing has taken place in the vicinity of Arnol.

Stock replacement is achieved by the rearing by the crofters of their own calves [sired in the 1940s by a Department of Agriculture for Scotland Ayrshire bull kept at the neighbouring township of Shawbost, and later by artificial insemination] and the stock is disposed of for sale as suckled calves or store cattle and cast cows.

In 1960, the stock of 42 Arnol amounted to one cow and calf, eight breeding ewes, three other sheep, and six lambs, with twenty poultry and six chickens. Since 1969, no cow or follower has been kept, and the sheep stock now comprises about twelve ewes and thirteen wethers, plus hoggs. The croft had only 0·4 ha of outrun, and had half a share in the common grazing. This meant that its 'souming' [the amount of stock allowed to be grazed by the Barvas Estate Ltd. in relation to the extent of the croft's arable] was one cow with one follower up to two years old, and seven sheep.

In order to keep a balance between crofters whose stock holding emphases varied, a system of equivalents was applied for working out the 'souming': 1 cow = 5 sheep; 1 horse = 2 cows or 10 sheep. No horses, however, are now kept in the township. The total area of the Arnol township common pasture amounts to 1672·6 ha, of which 16 ha were re-seeded in 1960 and 20 ha in 1961. This was held in 44 shares, ranging in size from half a share to two shares.

It is obvious that in districts such as this, where the sheep stocking rate is lower per 0·4 ha than in any other part of Scotland—except the most mountainous districts—and where in the neighbourhood of the crofts, turf cutting for the erection of dykes and the thatching of houses has led to considerable surface erosion and consequent impoverishment of the grazing, some degree of control is necessary to prevent overstocking and perhaps irreparable damage to the already poor pasture. For this reason regulations had to be applied and the first official attempt to this end was the Crofters Common Grazings Regulation Act of 1891. This was an almost complete failure, and a second Act was passed in 1908, which authorized, *inter alia*, the appointment of a Grazing Officer to assist in the administration under the Land Court and with power to summon, attend and advise any Grazing Committee [which was composed of local crofters]. The system still did not work well, and many people thought it would be simpler to revert to the old system of an unofficial township constable. However, the new Land Court created by the Small Landholders [Scotland] Act of 1911 was given unlimited powers to prescribe regulations binding on both crofters and non-crofters—the latter an important provision in view of the number of cottars on croft land and squatters on common pasture who held stock—and was also given complete control of the local administrative authority. It was empowered to appoint grazing committees composed in the way most appropriate for their district, and could apportion not only common grazings but also lands still held in runrig [jointly farmed], on application [Day, *Public Admin.*, 1918, pp. 196–200].

Essentially, the soumings are still looked after by a grazing committee, of which there is one for each township, and a clerk who has no executive or disciplinary power, and the general picture is very much as in 1955, when it was said that 'the situation now varies from law-abiding rigidity to complete neglect of the souming rules, which were originally made in the interests of conserving the grazings. The *coilpeachadh* or equating of one form of stock into another was originally intended to give flexibility, but in fact it has resulted in a widening of the cattle-sheep ratio, a phenomenon which . . . was not in the interest of conservation' [Darling, 1955, p. 207].

A tremendous amount of Central Government thought and activity has been expended on these areas following the nineteenth century development of public administration and the diminishing of the autocratic control of the estates. But in the more difficult areas, which include Arnol, the *status quo* is scarcely even being maintained. As in many areas of Lewis, depopulation is a serious problem. Agriculture is an increasingly minimal activity. The fishing industry has remained for the most part an east-coast prerogative, and though it provided a lot of employment for

West-side Lewismen, nevertheless it did so by taking them away from their crofts, leaving women, old folk and youngsters to carry on. Fishing is no longer of any importance for places like Arnol, though one or two men may go out line fishing for domestic supplies, and lobstering, on calm days. The home weaving industry which has been a useful source of income certainly keeps men at home, but it is difficult to be a full-time weaver and to work a croft fully at the same time.

The activities of the male population of Arnol fall into three main sections —service in the Merchant Navy, weaving, and crofting. In 1960, of a total male population of 82 between the ages of 15 and 65, 8 were full time crofters, 13 were weavers, and 12 were in the Merchant Navy. The remainder were unemployed, were working permanently away or were labouring for the Hydro Electricity Board. There were also two small shops catering for local needs.

In these respects Arnol is characteristic of West-side communities, but it also has its own distinctive marks. Physically, the rocky, stony ground has led to the erection of numerous dykes and Arnol has many more of these than comparable townships. More blackhouses have survived here than in most places, and this marks the tightly knit nature of the community, where between 1939–1960 only thirteen people are recorded as having left by migration. This is probably an understatement, however. There is little immigration through marriage. The Electoral Register for the township in 1960, for example, showed that a total voting population of 155 shared 12 surnames, among which Macleod was most common.

CROFTING TENURE

In 1962 the Scottish Land Court granted an application by the landlords, Barvas Estates Ltd., for authority to resume from crofting that area of No. 42 Arnol comprising the site of the blackhouse which the Ministry of Works, now the Department of the Environment, wished to preserve. The area was then feued by Barvas Estates Ltd. to the Ministry. This act of resumption was in keeping with crofting law.

Crofting law and crofting tenure was created by the Act of 1886 which followed the *Report of Her Majesty's Commissioners of Enquiry into the Condition of the Crofters and Cottars in the Highlands and Islands of Scotland.* The Commission that produced this report was set up, under the chairmanship of Lord Napier and Ettrick, as a result of the hardships and insecurity being suffered by small landholders and landless cottars following the complex of population movements known as the Highland Clearances. The Napier Commission Report and subsequent Crofters Holdings Act marked a turning-point in the history of the seven counties—Argyll, Inverness, Ross, Sutherland, Caithness, Orkney, and Shetland—to which they applied, with the Government becoming more and more the guardian of the Highlands. Since legislation is of a generalising nature, it tends to have a levelling effect in relation to local forms of social organisation and culture, so that in any investigation of the crofting areas it is necessary to understand the application and effects of legislation before trying to appreciate the situation prior to 1886.

The essential features of crofting tenure, established in that year, and still persisting, were:

1. Security of tenure so long as the crofter pays his rent and complies with a number of other conditions.

2. The right to a fair rent fixed, in the event of disagreement, by the Crofters Commission which was established by the Act of 1886. Fair rents are now fixed by the Scottish Land Court.

3. The right to compensation on leaving for permanent improvements provided by the crofter or the predecessor in the tenancy.

4. The right to bequeath the tenancy.

These four provisions still exist today although the original Act has from time to time been amended, extended, and modified. Although in some cases landlords provided the crofter's house, most croft houses were built by the crofters themselves. It is this aspect that has given the buildings of the crofting counties much of their varied regional character, for the individual crofters who built their own houses were inclined to stick to traditional building patterns and techniques.

The actual definition of a croft has also been altered in terms of area and of the amount of rent paid. The present limit is 29 ha of inbye land, or a rent not exceeding £50. It can be described as an agricultural unit, usually of small size, situated in the crofting counties and subject to the Crofters [Scotland] Acts. It comprises an area of inbye land around the buildings, in the exclusive occupation of the tenant, and in most but not all cases the tenant has a right to put his stock in common with other crofters in the township onto an area of common grazings. This communal aspect is an essential part of crofting.

At present there are approximately 18,500 crofts in the seven counties, tenanted by 15,500 crofters, of whom only 5% find full-time employment on their crofts. The others must find additions to their incomes from jobs like weaving, fishing, road work, and so on.

It is widely recognised that crofting tenure contains many anomalies. The chief of these is, as the Chairman of the Crofters' Commission, James Shaw Grant, put it, that a crofter is almost the only working man in Britain in the lower wage groups who is statutorily required to provide a house which he does not own in the normal sense of the word, which he cannot sell on the free market, and which he cannot use as security over a loan, since he does not own the solum. This aspect is now recognised as too rigid, and more restrictive than beneficial. It was this, inter alia, that led to the recommendations for reform in crofting tenure submitted by the Crofters' Commission to the Secretary of State in 1968, on the basis of which the Government's proposals were published in 1972 and the Crofters Reform [Scotland] Act became law in 1976.

This means that the crofting counties are standing on the threshold of what may well amount to a new revolution in the course of the next two or three decades. The general aim is to assimilate crofting into the ordinary legal structure of the country. The simple way to achieve this is by the conversion of crofting tenure into owner-occupancy, though whereas the Crofters' Commission advocated wholesale and compulsory conversion, the Government came down in favour of giving crofters an option.

The crofter will now have the possibility of freeing himself from many of his present restrictions. It will be possible for him to own his house and still remain a tenant of the land if he so wishes. It will also be possible for him to acquire a part of his land on a proper title if he wishes to develop, or to acquire the ownership of all his inbye land. However, if he wants to remain a crofter tenant he will still be able to share in the development value of any of his croft land which is resumed by his landlord. With the present legal restrictions that hinder development removed, crofters will for the first time be able to take advantage of the increasing development opportunities opening up in tourism and in other directions.

This Bill marks the second major phase in the legislative history of the crofting counties seen by the blackhouse at 42 Arnol.

Acknowledgements

I am greatly indebted for help and advice to Professor Ronald Miller, for data from the Crofting Survey carried out by the Dept. of Geography of the University of Glasgow; to J. R. Spence of the Crofters' Commission; to A. Jones of the North of Scotland College of Agriculture; and to several individuals including Dr. J. Caird, J. M. Macmillan, K. Smith and the late Angus Gillies.

SOURCES

Confidential Reports to the Secretary for Scotland on the Condition of the Western Highlands and Islands, October, 1886

Darling, F. Fraser, *Crofting Agriculture*, Edinburgh and London, 1945

Darling, F. Fraser, *West Highland Survey*, Oxford, 1956

Day, J. P., *Public Administration in the Highlands and Islands of Scotland*, London, 1918

Evidence Taken by Her Majesty's Commissioners of Enquiry into the Condition of Crofters and Cottars in the Highlands and Islands of Scotland, Edinburgh, 1884

The First Statistical Account of Scotland, Vol. XIX, Edinburgh, 1797

Geddes, A., *The Isle of Lewis and Harris*, Edinburgh, 1955

Land Use in the Highlands and Islands. Report submitted by The Advisory Panel on The Highlands and Islands to the Secretary of State for Scotland on 27 October 1964

MacLeoid, T., 'Tigh Còmhnaidh An Innse—Gall' in *Gairm*, No. 32, 1962

New Statistical Account of Scotland, Vol. XIV, London, 1845

Notes of Evidence Taken by the Commissioners appointed to Enquire into Certain Matters Affecting the Interests of the Population of the Western Highlands and Islands of Scotland, London, 1891

Report of Her Majesty's Commissioners of Inquiry into the Condition of the Crofters and Cottars in the Highlands and Islands of Scotland, Edinburgh, 1884

Report to Her Majesty's Secretary for Scotland on the Condition of the Cottar Population in the Lews, 1888

Report to the Local Government Board for Scotland on the Burden of the Existing Rates and the General Financial Position of the Outer Hebrides, 1906

Report to the Secretary for Scotland by The Crofters on the Social Condition of the People of Lewis in 1901, as compared with Twenty Years Ago, 1902

The West Side Story, Shawbost School, May, 1964

Ancient Monuments and Historic Buildings

Many ancient sites and buildings are maintained as national monuments by the Department of the Environment.

Guide-books and postcards are on sale at many monuments and are also obtainable from the bookshops of Her Majesty's Stationery Office, or from the Ancient Monuments Publications Section, Department of the Environment, Argyle House, Lady Lawson Street, Edinburgh EH3 9SD, (Chief Information Officer, Department of the Environment, 2 Marsham Street, London, SW1, for English and Welsh monuments).

Photographs of most monuments may be obtained in large prints at commercial rates, plus postage, from the Photographic Librarian, Department of the Environment, Argyle House, Lady Lawson Street, Edinburgh EH3 9SD, (Photographic Librarian, Department of the Environment, Hannibal House, London, SE1, for English and Welsh monuments).

Season tickets, valid for 12 months from date of issue, admitting their holders to all ancient monuments and historic buildings in the care of the State in Scotland, England and Wales, may be obtained from the Department of the Environment or at many monuments.